NATIONAL LAMPOON'S
Truly Sick, Tasteless, and Twisted Cartoons

Contemporary Books

Chicago   New York   San Francisco   Lisbon   London   Madrid   Mexico City
Milan   New Delhi   San Juan   Seoul   Singapore   Sydney   Toronto

Contemporary Books

A Division of The **McGraw·Hill** *Companies*

1 2 3 4 5 6 7 8 9 0 VGR/VGR 0 9 8 7 6 5 4 3 2 1

ISBN 0-07-139029-4

These cartoons have been previously published in regular and special editions of *National Lampoon*® magazine.

Printed and bound by Victor Graphics
Cover design by Todd Petersen

This book is printed on acid-free paper.

"Hey, want to see some sewage?"

Bob the Frog

"Romulus is going to found Rome and Remus is going to become a pimp."

"Gesundheit!"

"... And then we have the 'Terrorist Special' where you're shot
in the head and then dumped at the airport of your choice."

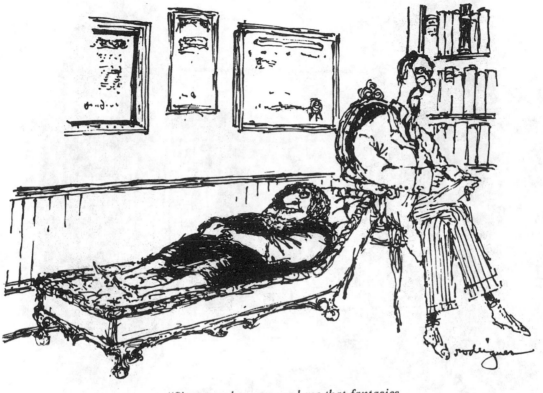

"Since you have assured me that fantasies
are quite normal, Doctor, I'll describe one
in particular that gives me immense pleasure.
My husband is lying in bed nude while a beautiful
young girl is squatting just above his face. He slowly
raises his head to her pubic area, and
I hit them both with a flamethrower!"

"*Well, I hope you're satisfied. Now you've scared the others away.*"

"Shall I wait up for you?"

"Let me through! I'm an upholsterer!"

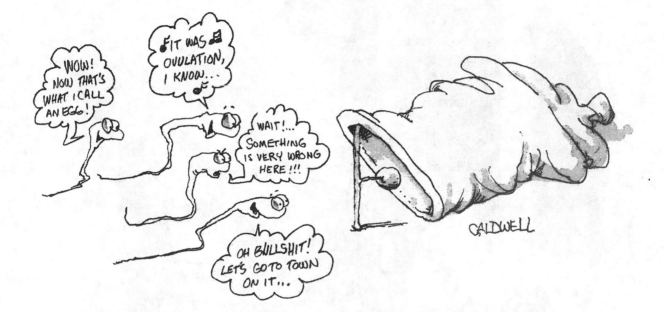

"Just as I thought. This mummy has a 'curse'!"

"*My brother Bruce wants to know if you would blow him instead of the house.*"

"Chief, I don't like to tell you how to run your department, but it's an election year and the unions are raising hell with me, so from now on, when electrodes are applied to prisoners' genitals, it's gotta be done by union electricians only!"

"How many times have
I told you not to leave crumbs in the bed?"

"I'm sorry, sir, but I've got to ask you another question. I heard someone in the courtroom shout out the correct answer."

*"No one's been sleeping in my bed, but my tennis
racket smells like tuna fish!"*

PCVEY

WOULD I BE PROUD TO SERVE THIS TO MY OWN FAMILY?
WOULD I BE PROUD TO SERVE THIS TO MY OWN FAMILY?
WOULD I
ACE POULTRY

"MY WIFE AND MY BEST FRIEND.
HOW COULD I HAVE BEEN SO BLIND?"

"Well and good, gentlemen. But do you think the enemy will be using such tiny ships?"

"Today I am a man!"

P.C.Vey

"If I were you I'd go to the country for a while...but then I have a half-million-dollar estate with two swimming pools and three tennis courts to go to and you don't, so maybe you'd better stay home."

MANKOFF

"Excuse me for interrupting, madam, but before you go on allow me to make these comments: one, I have no desire for you to do my cooking; two, I neither want nor need you to pay my rent; three, I'm very sorry you cried the whole night long; and four, and perhaps most important, I think you've called the wrong Bill Bailey."

"*Mister, want these rubbers?*"

"In a minute! In a minute!"

"Damn it! I just stepped in wolf shit!"

"Darling, we can't go on meeting like this. My husband is starting to get suspicious."

"So far so good, but now what are we going to do
about the burglar alarm in my vagina?"

*"You should have phoned, Mr. Broughton—
Glenda's not here this week. She's working skid row
while she has her period."*

"Boy! That was either the best head or the best ass I've ever had!"

"Well, how was I supposed to know you were saving them for something special?"

"So carpentry wasn't good enough for Mr. Big Shot?"

"Psst. Hey, mister, I got a message for your mayor. Tell him there's a plague of frogs camped just off Astoria in Queens. Tell him to cough up ten thousand gallons of flies or he won't even begin to know the meaning of the word trouble."

"*My goodness, Grandmother...what an exceptionally large clitoris you have!*"

"Hey, John! Instead of giving you a haircut, this time I thought I'd just blow your fucking head off."

"We're going to have to prepare her Manhattan rather than New England style. She's having her period."

"It's your mother and she's covered with flies and shit. Should I let her in?"

"Snailman! Thank heavens!"

"Here we are, I'll put in your fifty cents. Okay, here we go. Oh boy, this looks like a real sizzler. It shows this girl on a bed with only panties on—wow! What a pair of knockers on her! A guy is walkin' over to her and he's unzipping his fly, now she starts takin' her panties off and he..."

"If you're ever sick or anything and your secretary needs some papers signed, I can do your signature perfectly."

"Let's faunicate."

"NONE OF THE GUYS DOWN AT THE HOME FOR THE
BLIND WILL BELIEVE THAT I SLEPT WITH BO DEREK!"

"Ingemar has always marched to the beat of a different drummer."

"C'mon, Winky....Bad enough it's a slow corner, but I'll never sell any pencils if you keep humping my leg!"

"Maybe he can't swim."

"Yes. I have a question. Will we
get a chance to fuck a horse?"

S. GROSS

"...And we were able to survive the two and a half hours that we were stuck between the eighth and ninth floors by drinking our own urine."

E. SUBITZKY

"Hey, Dad, can I have the car tonight?"

S. GROSS

"Second question: This is the first time I've ever gone down on a perfect stranger—true or false?"

"Hey, how about a vegetable?"

"Of course, the original pendulum kept better time."

"You know, I'd be out of business if it weren't for self-destructive perverted bastards like you."

"He followed me home, mom. Can I eat him?"

"I am not a scale. I am a Martian.
You are standing on my testicles."

S.GROSS

"Well! I think this calls for a little drink."

"Madam, I think one of the reasons you're not satisfied with your vibrator is that you expect too much from it."

"Did you see where I put my goddam nuts?"

"Not all of us are like this. I have a problem with premature ejaculation."

S. GROSS

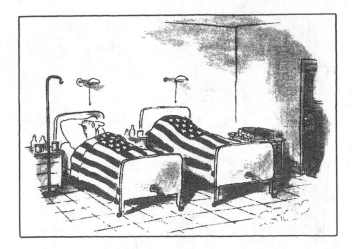

"Oh, wow, like where do you get your ideas?"

90

"No need to pay me, madam—I'll just sniff the monkey's finger."

"*I guess we never should have gotten married, eh, sis?*"

"Doctor, this is Mr. Gusset. Mr. Gusset thinks he's the Empire State Building."

"Bless me, Father, for I have sinned...."

"Say, buddy, you got any idea where
the Illiterate Club is?"

"I'm sorry, the parents of the young man in that wreck
refuse to donate his liver. They are, however, giving me
an excellent deal on parts for my Porsche."

"Which do you prefer—sharing a room with a person who's slightly out of his mind from heavy medication, or a room with a person who's throwing up all the time?"

"Be careful, dear, it might be poisonous."

"What if I was to give you a choice, Helen. . . . I can say I'm sorry for being insensitive to your needs and not taking your feelings about our relationship seriously, whereupon we make up and possibly even conclude the discussion with lovemaking. . . or I could just take a .357 magnum and paint the wall with your spoiled-little-white-bitch brains."

Carl Gets Up on the Wrong Side of the Bed for the Last Time.

"My compliments to the chef!"

"*Well, well, Heffernan! Associate editor at* Harper's... *managing editor at the* Atlantic... *a nice stint with the* Times Book Review... *May I say how pleased we are to have you here at* Oriental Wet Snatch Illustrated*!*"

SIBERIAN STATIC TORTURE.

"*I suppose this means we won't be able to go to school today?*"

"I'm doing one hell of a business with the S and M crowd."

"Al's a nice guy and everything, but never bone his wife, molest his children, and burn down his house all in the same day."

PLEASE
HELP
PROMISING
FOOTBALL
CAREER
CUT SHORT
DUE TO A
SEVERE
GROIN INJURY

CALDWELL

E. SUBITZKY

"According to this there's nothing wrong with you... but then these are the papers to my house and car."

"The job doesn't pay very much, but I make it up to you by letting you sniff the seats."

"Where ya goin', wimp? A real man can <u>hold</u> his urine."

"No, I'm not expecting a child. On the contrary, I just ate one."

"*No kidding—Stottlemeyer's date's got twelve tits.*"

127

"Oh, Cecil, Cecil, Cecil... if only you'd read the instructions that came with your chain saw!"

"Oh! He must be sick."

"Mr. Hallet, if we could put one of your hemorrhoids on this safety pin as bait, there's a good chance we could catch a fish."

"Wake up, Woofey! I have to make a good impression on this job interview!"

"Yes, I can well imagine that it's not easy to whistle anymore, but give yourself time, Mr. Chase."

"More! Please, more! Oh, I've been such a naughty, handsome, enchanted prince!"

"I'm not hungry. I just want to look up her dress."

S GROSS

"Is he…dead?"

"It's a telegram from the governor.... 'Happy birthday to you.... Happy birthday to you.... Happy birthday, dear...'"

"Nice dog you got there, mister! Drop a quarter in the cup or else my monkey squeezes his balls."

"…Castration knife… castration knife… castration knife…"

"Sorry, no, but if you folks ever get up around Merton-Indiana way, you come by to supper with Mother and me."

"Et tu, Bruce?"

"I'll be frank with you, Charlene. I've used my body to get what I wanted."

A VISIT TO GRANDFATHER'S ALLIGATOR FARM

"Good evening. I've run out of gas. Would it be too much of an imposition for you and your lovely wife to step out into the street and push my car to a gas station?"

"Hey, Marlene, be a doll and stick this zucchini in your ass and show Ned your *Jimmy Durante imitation*."

"Don't lecture me on civil rights, Mr. Wilbur—you forfeited your civil rights when you came in my mouth down at the bus station."

"What's the matter, Lassie—is Timmy in trouble?"

"*The stitches can come out in seven or eight days, and I see no reason why you can't begin denying him sex in about two weeks.*"

"WHEELS? Fischer Bros. doesn't sell WHEELS!"

"Butchie's asleep, you should have no trouble with him. The first switch is the porch light. The one in the middle's for the living room, and this one will suck the face right off your skull. There's pizza in the fridge; we'll be home by eleven."

"It's not necessary to call Simmons in, Mr. Mount. I can take him out from here."

"Piss on me and you're dead."

S.GROSS

"There was an eighth dwarf, 'Lumpy,' but he died of cancer."

"We'll have to get a new bird, Mary. This one just isn't cleaning up the lice, dandruff, and dried skin the way it used to."

"Hello, boys, I'm Mister Rogers! Don't be frightened, I won't kill you."

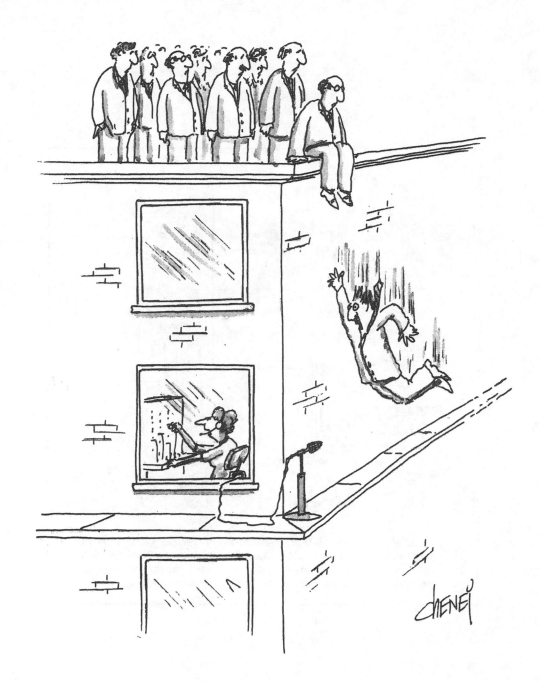

"At the tone, the time will be…"

"Good afternoon, sir. I'm Dr. Leonard Delray of Proctology Associates, Inc., down at the Busy Pilgrim Mall. As part of our Midsummer Wackiness Sale, we're giving door-to-door free estimates. So if you'll kindly bend over and spread them, we can start you on the road to affordable proctology service."

"We have to talk."

*"All right, all right—I'm sure you've all seen
somebody gettin' an enema before..."*

CALDWELL

"Fongu!"

"You really took Muffy and Scott and Todd down to the lake and let them go...
honest? Have you got a note or something from them so I could be sure?"

"I said, 'Eat your fucking vegetables, you scum-sucking pig.' What did you think I said?"

"Pass it on down the line: 'Anyone who plays with her tits will never see the promised land.'"

THE BIRTH OF A LEGEND

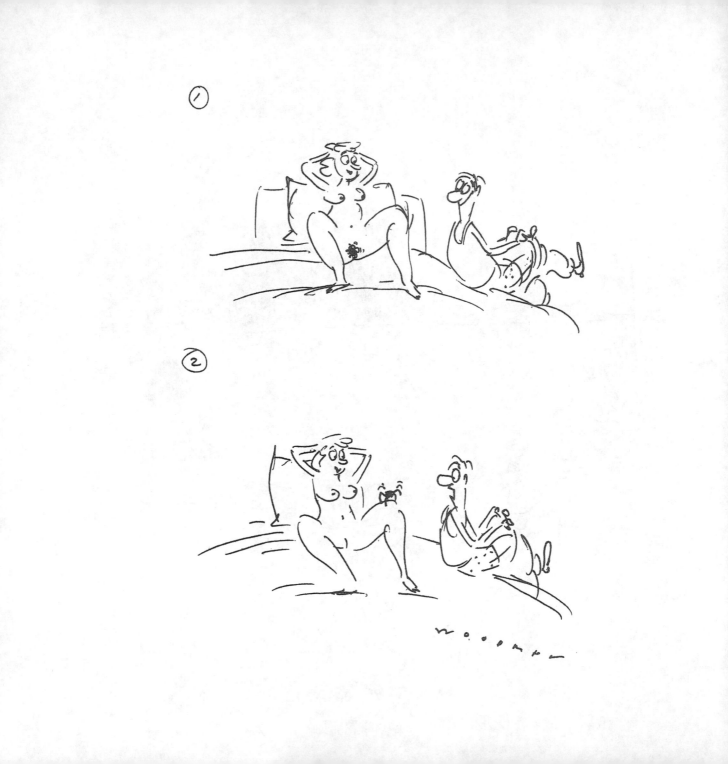

"Can I call you back, Ted? Half of my desk just exploded, some people are throwing shit at my window, and my secretary has been abusing her medication."

"Darling, we can't go on meeting like this. He's due to be wormed next week."

"Ticket, please."

LEO Cullum

"I'm from the IRS. I'm afraid we've misused all your tax money.
Could we have some more?"

"I'll give you five bucks if you let me sniff your cart."

"Mama, get help! I jerked it right off!"

"Don't take it so hard, Billy. I'm sure even professional ballplayers sometimes shit their pants when they're sliding into second."

"I wouldn't say that jerking off ten times a day is a health risk, but maybe you should use your left hand once in a while."

"*Excuse me…the missus wants to know if you folks would like to stay for dinner.*"

"Pssst, c'mere...there's another peephole over here!"

"Beatrice, over here! Peas the size of your brain! No exaggeration."

"You have only to glance at my wife's intimate undergarments and I shall be forced to kill you."

"Quick! Make fun of the size of his genitals and perhaps he'll retreat in embarrassment!"

S. GROSS

*"And I tell you I searched desperately for a black elf! A Jewish elf! A female elf!
The only break I've gotten is that most elves are gay!"*

*"Maurice, show Irene and Joe the funny trick
you do with your colostomy bag."*

"Is this it, Edward? Is this as kinky as we're going to get?"

"Offhand I'd say you have an excellent case, Mr. Vogel. How long ago was this autopsy performed on you?"

"Oh, no! My best friend and my best friend's wife!"

"Be careful! This soup is so hot, it's still bubbling!"

"Did anyone ever tell you you have body odor?"

"We are a very poor country, and we can't afford to buy electrodes for your testicles."

"Do you have something for the control of premature ejac...ooo...ooo... ooooohhh.... Never mind."

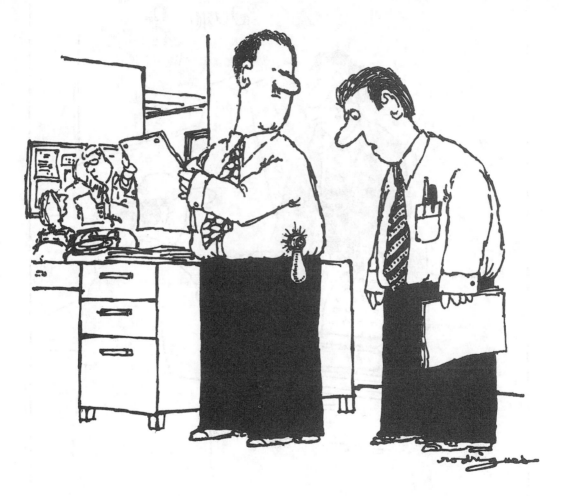

"Herb, who did you say the doctor was who did your colostomy?"

"*His prostate is just fine!*"

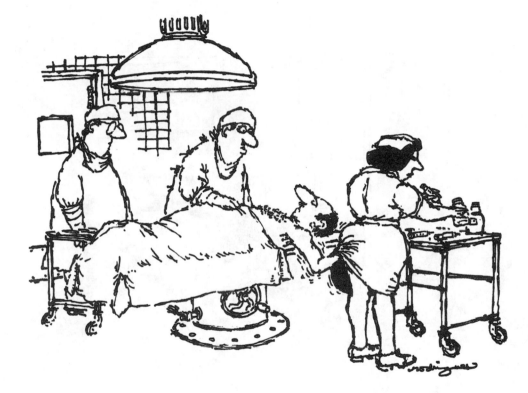

"Mr. Guzman, are you quite sure that you want to go through with this sex-change operation?"

*"Did you know that 'getting fixed' means
having your balls cut off?"*

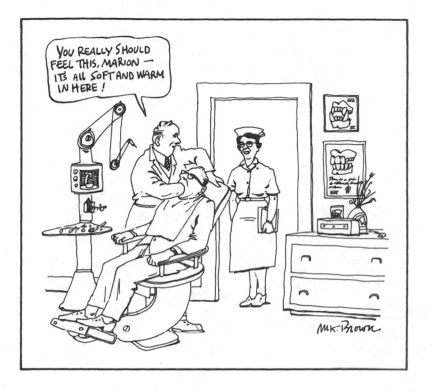

"Don't pick those. Those are dingleberries."

"And while you're waiting for your order, don't forget to check out our free salad bar."

SEE
THE BUGS
OF
NEW-YORK
25¢

S.GROSS

"Send Orgill in, will you? I have something I'd like to bounce off him."

"Wait! Come back! I don't even know your name!"

"*I left my wife this morning. Of course, it was only to go to work, but I feel good about it.*"

"Do you get this joke, Harold? I don't. Do you understand this new humor, Harold? I don't. I just don't get it. Do you, Harold?"

"Apple pie! This isn't a trick, is it?"

"Our only hope is for them to reach a quick climax."

"Okay, all those in favor of taking to the streets, signify by saying 'Aye.'"

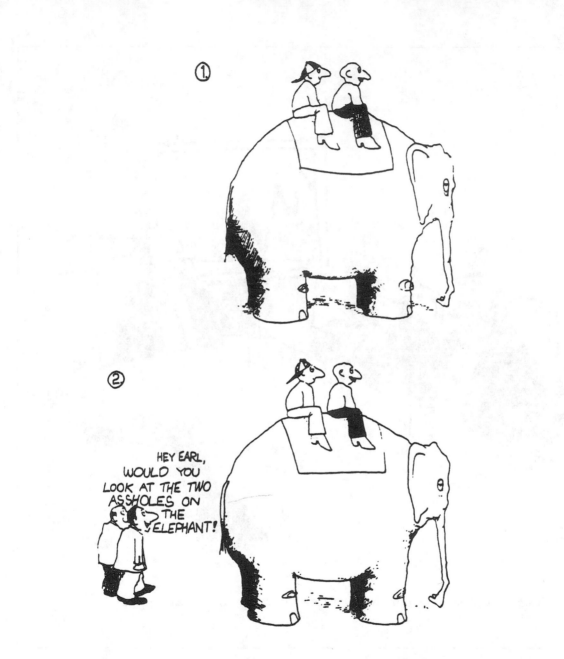

③

④

"Someone's been sleeping in my bed, and what's more, she neglected to use a sanitary napkin!"

The original design for Barney the Dinosaur didn't go over well.

"Okay—which one of us is talking now?"

"Whose dead cat is that hanging on the clothesline?"

21

Snake suicides

23

"YOU WORK TOO HARD, BONDS. YOU SHOULD TAKE TIME TO STOP AND SMELL THE ASSHOLES."

"He looks like he's just about to come!!! You guys ready?!?"

"It's like this, son—a man's gotta do what a man's gotta do!"

"This is a great little place. I took my last wife here and she choked on a bone and died."

P.C.VEY

"Hopefully you won't have anything to worry about tonight.
Robert's mother made him jerk off twice before he left the house."

"–and I'll have the 'no justice, no peace' with a side of red beans and rice."

"It's a free record insert . . . 'Music to Jerk Off By'!"

"Hey, Grandma! Remember when I was little
and you used to make sure my scarf was wrapped nice and tight?
Well, who's doing the tightening now, Grandma?! . . . Who's doing the tightening now?!"

37

"TAKE YOUR ORDER, SIR?"

"And what did my little darling do in school today?"

42

"This report needs work, Miss Shulman. I suggest we roll up
our sleeves, uncross our legs, and get down to business."

"Tri-corder readings indicate the presence of hot bitches, Captain!"

"You have a great wife, Al. . . . How often does she get stuck in that window?"

48

"C'mon, Motormouth, read Birdbrain another subtitle and chuckle your amusing little chuckle!"

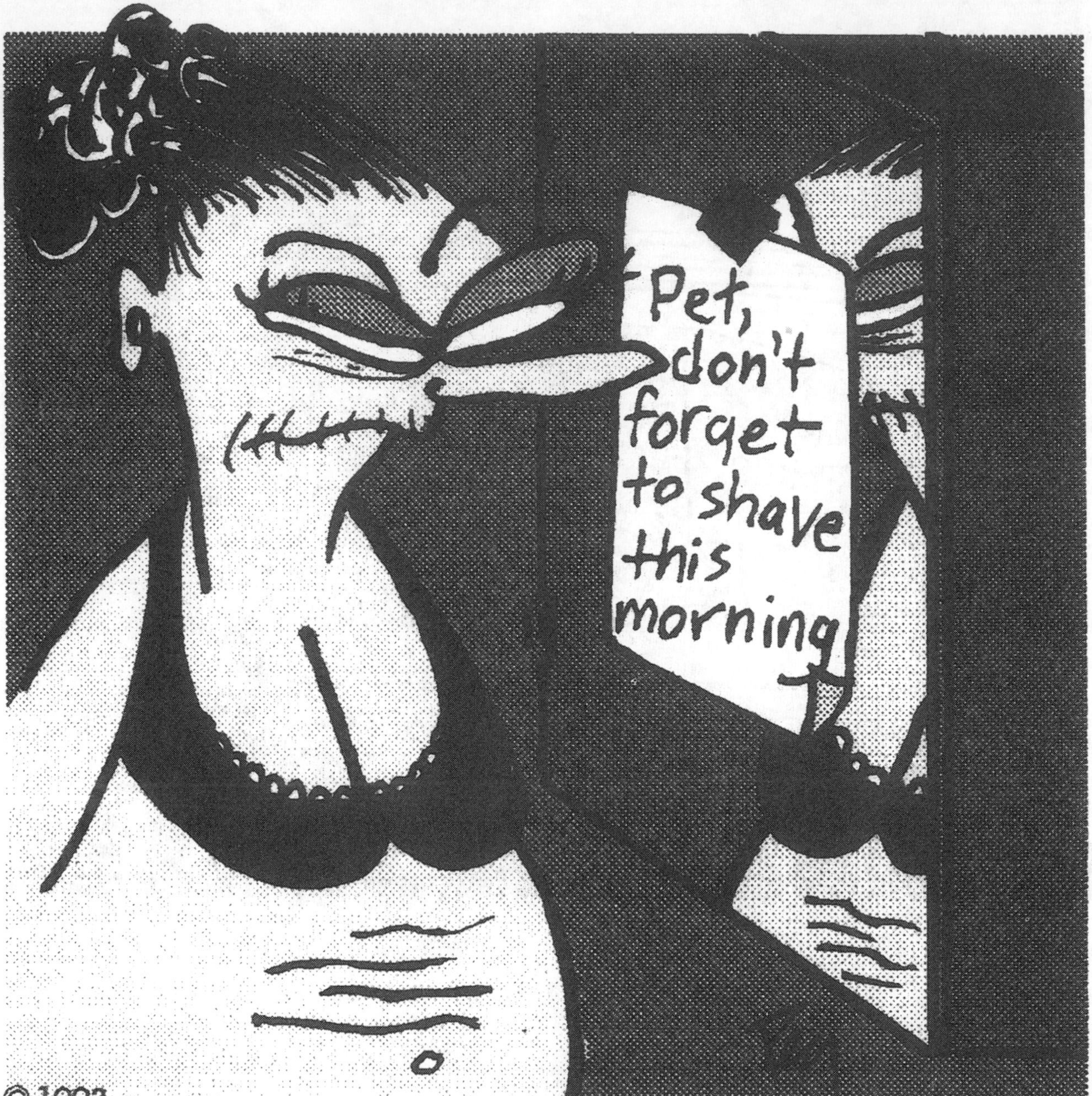
Pet, don't forget to shave this morning
©1993

"He eats from the garbage, he could sleep in the garage, and his wine costs only ninety-eight cents a bottle. Oh please, Daddy, please, can we keep him?"

"The thing I resent is that he's taken all the gay trade from us."

"You see? God is punishing us
because you bought futures in pork bellies."

BARTACUS YOU IDIOT! I SAID MY NAME WAS BARTACUS!

"I don't mean to alarm you, but your kid just boned me up the ass and now he's rimming the cat."

"We make our choices . . . butcher, baker, or candlestick maker . . . and we live with them. Right, Arnie?"

"I had a jar of mint jelly in my rucksack and now it's gone.
Do you want to talk about it?"

"Okay, a quick and merciful death. Now, what's your second wish, Mr. Thompson? Mr. Thompson . . . Mr. Thompson . . . ?"

69

75

"Did you get a smell of her feet?"

"If it makes you feel any better, your wife was a lousy lay."

"Heck, no! We're not crazy! Why? Do we look crazy?"

...THEN THE LITTLE PIG WHO BUILT HIS HOUSE OF STRAW GOT A FEDERAL DISASTER GRANT AND BUILT HIS HOUSE OF STRAW ALL OVER AGAIN.

"I've always thought it was eerie. He expired the same day as his Visa card."

"WE'RE NOT BAPTISTS, WE'RE FLOOD VICTIMS"

"Too bad we won't live another ten years. By then, women probably won't even be wearing bikinis."

Pigs in Love

"And you, Al, what's new with you?"

"Hey, you're right, Inspector Peterson, they are *all ant farms."*

"How was I supposed to know that the apple was a controlled substance?"

"Me too . . . I'm an oppressed dissident novelist being kept here for political reasons. Now can I eat one of your boogers???"

"I really don't need any magazines. How about locks, do you have any locks?"

"Hello, Stromboli Pizza? When you deliver the Deckers' pizza, could you bring a small pie with anchovies to the white van parked in front of their house?"

"There used to be an eighth dwarf, Humpy, but he left rather suddenly."

"I was going to give you three months. But since the prisons are all full, I guess I'll have to sentence you to death."

CRAZY MOM

106

CALDWELL

"Rachel, meet Bob. Bob was just telling me how much he'd like to
stick his filthy penis down your throat
till you choke. . . But I assume he was only joking."

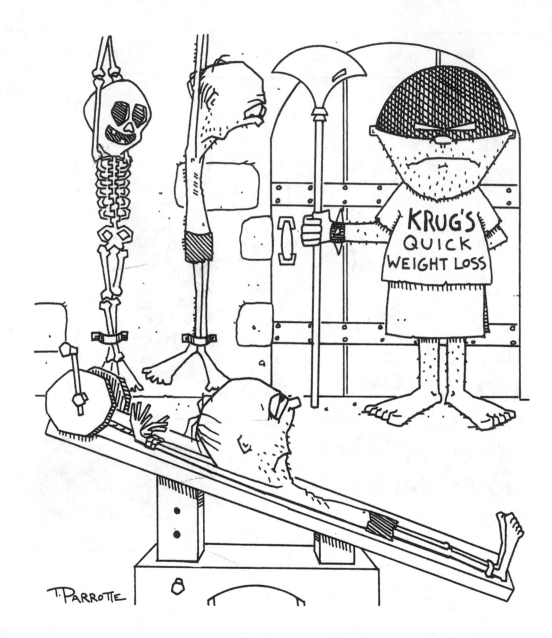

THE **MALAYSIAN RUBBER SNAKE** SHEDS ITS SKIN SEASONALLY.

"Don't worry—he's dead."

"What's this I hear about you dressing up like a woman and blowing me in the bathroom?"

"SO LONG. I'LL MISS YOU!"

"Not tonight, dear. You've gained fifty pounds and lost most of your hair."

"Next time, think twice before mooning a werewolf."

"And he was making such progress."

"I think it's cat fur."

"Don't worry, sweetie, I didn't even look at another woman.
All I did was lie in the sun and get a tan."

"GERALD NEVER COULD TIE A DOUBLE WINDSOR!"